The Bear

A Play

Anton Chekhov

A SAMUEL FRENCH ACTING EDITION

SAMUEL
FRENCH

FOUNDED 1830

SAMUELFRENCH-LONDON.CO.UK
SAMUELFRENCH.COM

ISBN 978-0-573-12016-9

www.samuelfrench-london.co.uk

www.samuelfrench.com

FOR AMATEUR PRODUCTION ENQUIRIES

UNITED KINGDOM AND WORLD
EXCLUDING NORTH AMERICA
plays@SamuelFrench-London.co.uk
020 7255 4302/01

Each title is subject to availability from Samuel French,

depending upon country of performance.

THE BEAR

First performed at The King's Head, Islington,
London, N1 with the following cast :

Flora McNeil	Maslen George
Leckie	David Smidman
Andrew Baird	Richard Baker

The play was directed by **Bernard Lawrence**

CHARACTERS

Flora McNeil, an attractive widow
Andrew Baird, a wealthy landowner
Leckie, an old servant

The action of the play takes place in Flora's house in Glasgow

Time: 1890

PRODUCTION NOTE

The Director has a choice of either an imaginary casement window DC, with imaginary curtains—or a practical window and curtains UC. The business of drawing back the curtains, opening the windows and shouting to the street occurs on page 9.

B.L.

THE BEAR

The living-room of a large house on the outskirts of Glasgow. It is a hot afternoon in summer, in 1890. There is a desk and chair, a table and a chaise longue

If front tabs are used, as the CURTAIN *rises Mrs McNeil is seated at the desk. She is beautiful, in black, gazing at a photograph in a heavy black frame. Leckie, a manservant, is clearing a table. He is obviously upset*

If no tabs are used, Mrs McNeil enters from UR, *moves to the desk, sits, and gazes at the photo for a moment, then Leckie enters from* UL *and starts clearing the cup, saucer and plate from the table*

Leckie Madam, I've tried to hold my tongue—I have tried—but it's no use, I must speak. Ye canna go on like this—you're just ruining yourself. D'ye no ken it's Fairs Week? Everybody's out enjoying themselves—the banks are closed, and the shops—the city's empty. Even the cat's lying in the sun catching wee flies—but for you, madam, today's just another day, ye just sit and greet. It's been like this for a whole year. You never go out of the house except to the Kirk on Sundays. There ye sit, day in, day out—looking at that picture or playing hymns on the harmonium—and you only know two!

Flora Mr Leckie, as I have said many times before, I shall never go out. Why should I? I feel that my own life came to an end when my dear, dear husband was laid to rest. We are both, as you might say, dead.

Leckie Och, that's no the way to go on. Ay, your man is dead—it's the will of the Lord, may his soul rest in peace. And as ye should, you've mourned him for him—but no for a whole year. I mind well when my own wife passed on—I was heartbroken, ay, heartbroken. I swear I wept for two days, mebbe three—but then I said to myself "That's enough". Then a wonderful thing happened. I suddenly realized how peaceful it was when she was no there! Of course, *I* had no mind tae marry again—but it'll be different with you, no doubt. You're yet young and a bonnie lassie—but mind well—beauty doesna last. In ten years' time, ye'll perhaps not be wearing so well. You'll have missed your chances.

Flora Mr Leckie, I shall never marry again. When my husband died as a result of his terrible accident, you mind very well I made a solemn promise that until the end of my days I would wear mourning and shut myself away from the world. It will be some consolation to me that if his spirit is with us, he will see what a devoted wife I am——

Leckie For goodness sakes! I'm mebbe saying what I shouldna—but did he no used to knock you about?

Flora I'll admit he did.

Leckie Was he not the most miserly hypocrite that ever shamed the kilt?

Flora He did not spend freely.

Leckie Did he no spend freely enough on loose women?

Flora He did have his little faults, I'll admit. He fell from grace.

Leckie Ay, he fell right enough. He fell, dead drunk from the battlements of Edinburgh Castle. I wonder who it was that had the good sense tae push him?

Flora That will do, Leckie!

The doorbell rings

Answer the door—and remember I see no-one.

Leckie exits UL

(*To the picture*) Oh, Neil McNeil—I hope you can see that I know how to behave. You neglected me, ill treated me—left me for days at a time. But as I often told you, I am a woman of breeding and so I am obliged to forgive you. And I hope that makes you thoroughly ashamed of yourself! (*She puts the picture down and moves to recline on the* chaise longue)

Leckie enters UL

Leckie Madam, there's a man to see you.

Flora Did you not tell him that I am in mourning for my poor dear husband?

Leckie That I did. He wouldn'a listen. He's stamping about in a terrible temper. He says it's very urgent.

Flora Show him out.

Leckie You've no seen him, madam. He's six foot tall and built like a wall. And I know him. It's Andrew Baird.

Flora And who might he be?

Leckie Have ye no heard tell of Andrew Baird? Och, he's a terrible bully! Everyone calls him "The Bear"! Ay, a great bear of a man!

Andrew Baird enters UL

Baird *You*! Ay—*you*! Have ye no told her I'm in a hurry? Och, awa' out wi' ye!

Leckie exits UL

It's Mrs Neil McNeil, is it no? I'm Andrew Baird, ex-Regimental Sergeant Major, Black Watch. I now own three estates in the Trossachs and unless you can sort out a wee matter of business, I may have to sell one of them to stay out of prison!

Flora What has this to do with me? I don't even know you.

Baird Ay, but your late husband did. And your late husband as ye well know was a wee bit canny when it came to paying what he owed—and my God! He certainly owed me!

Flora Am I to understand my husband died in debt to you? If you will kindly lower your voice and tell me the precise amount, I will pay you. How much was it?

Baird Five hundred and fifty pounds, ten shillings and sixpence. Here's his note. (*He produces the note*) And I need it *now*!

Flora But my good man—I haven't got that sort of money about the house. And since the banks are closed today, there's no way I can get it for you now. Besides, in my state of mind I cannot bear to think of such things.

Baird And in my "state of mind" I cannot bear to think of going to prison! Because that's where my creditors will put me if I don't pay them!

Flora Well, as I have said, sir, I cannot pay you now. I will pay you on Tuesday.

Baird It's no good on Tuesday. I want it *now*!!

Flora I'm exceedingly sorry—it's quite impossible.

Baird And "it's quite impossible" to wait!

Flora I have not got such a large amount about my person.

Baird You mean you'll no pay?

Flora That is correct.

Baird And that's your last word?

Flora It is, most definitely—and kindly make some effort to control your dreadful temper.

Baird Everyone keeps saying that to me. It's no my fault I've got a temper. All the polis keep saying is "Andrew Baird, why do you no learn to control your temper?" Well, I'll tell you—I lose my temper because of unreasonable people. I'm a perfectly reasonable man—why should I no lose my temper when you refuse to pay me money? (*He shouts*) I need that money! Yesterday I went to all the others who owe me money—people I had been kind enough to help out when they were in trouble—and would you believe it? Not one of them paid up! So then I remembered you— and what do you say? You haver on about your "state of mind". What about the state of my bank balance? Why *shouldn't* I be angry? Jings! Ye great daft woman—what have ye got for brains? God send me strength!

Flora How dare you speak to me like this?

Baird Och, I'm sorry. But "state of mind" for God's sake! "State of mind" my foot!! Have I got to pay my debts on Monday or have I not? Have I or have I not? Och, it's fine for you—your old man kicks the bucket—so you've got this "state of mind". That's all very well for you, is it no? What about me? I'm no married—my wife hasn't died, so what do I do? I can't have a convenient "state of mind", can I? I've got to pay up, haven't I? My whole business is about to be knocked down with me underneath—unless of course my creditors will take your "state of mind" on account! I know what I'll do—I'll go and ding my head against a brick wall! That't would be better than what I did yesterday. I go to MacGregor, and he's "no very well the day"; McKenzie's "gone fishing"; I couldn't get a penny out of Campbell—even after I'd thrown him through the window! And all the others are awa' tae Rothesay! And you, you have a "state of mind". Not one of you will pay up. And for why? I'll tell you why—because I'm too easy with the lot of you. I'm too soft, too well-balanced, too understanding! Well, I understand this much—I've got to get tougher. I'll tell you what I'm going to do with you—I'm going to stay right here until you *do* pay up! (*He shouts off*) You!! (*He moves towards the door* UL)

Leckie enters UL

Ay, you!
Leckie Ay, sir. Here I am.
Baird Bring me a whisky. A large one!

Leckie quickly exits UL

For God's sake! A "state of mind"! Just like a woman. That's why I keep well away from women now. Women? I'd rather be smoking on top of a barrel of gunpowder than talk to one of them. Och, they may play the fine lady, but they dinna fool me for a minute. Oh, Johnny Knox—he kent it well—"The monstrous regiment of women". God help us puir wee men!

Leckie enters UL *with whisky*

Leckie Mr Baird, sir—madam is no well—she can't see anyone.
Baird Oh, that's why I can't get any sense out of her—she can't see
me. I'm invisible! Mrs McNeil, I'm standing here. (*He sits L of the
chaise longue*) Now I'm sitting here—and here I'll stay. I'll stay
a week if I have to. Jings! I'll stay a year!! And it's no use trying
to get out of it—and you can't get round me because you've got
a pretty face and pretty eyes and because black suits you so well.
(*He feels round his collar*) Och, I'm sweating—it's too damned
hot! *You*! More whisky—and make it bigger. And bring it *on the
double*! (*He rise and moves towards Leckie*)

Leckie exits UL

What a day! I'm hot and I'm sweating and I'm dirty—I've been
rushing about to get what's owed to me—dealing with crooks and
welshers. So, if it upsets you, you've only got yourself to blame.
(*He starts to take off his coat*)

Leckie enters UL

Leckie You go too far, sir!
Baird What? *What*? Go too far? Don't you speak to me like that or
you'll go too far—through yon window!
Leckie Jings! He's mad!
Baird What did you say?
Leckie Not a word, sir.
Baird Away and hang up my coat. (*He throws the coat at him*) And
don't crease it!

Leckie exits UL

You know, you shouldn't let servants talk like that to your guests.
He's upset me again. Just when I was calming down. Och, I'm
furious—I could smash up the place!!
Flora Would you be so good as to lower your voice. It's not a thing
I'm used to.

Baird And I'm no used to being cheated.

Flora I have given you my word that I will pay you on Tuesday, have I not?

Baird And I've told you I want the money now, have I not? And I'll tell you something else—if you don't pay me today—I'll shoot myself. I'm a crack shot—I never miss!!

Flora In that case, I'll not detain you. (*She moves towards the door* UR)

Baird What? Och, ay, of course—it'd suit you just fine if I shot myself, would it no? Ay, thst would get you out of it altogether. Well, you can forget it. Here I am and here I stay—and I'm no joking.

Flora You're shouting again.

Baird *Who's shouting!?*

They stand nose to nose

Flora *You are!!*

Baird *And so too are you!!*

Flora You have no idea how to behave in the company of a lady.

Baird I don't know how to behave?

Flora No, sir, you do not.

Baird *Me?* Not know how to behave? For God's sake!! You've got a bloody nerve!!

Flora I do not care for your language, sir.

Baird And what's wrong with my language? Am I no speaking English? Perhaps you'd prefer it in French—or German—or in your case, Double Dutch!

Flora That was a stupid remark.

Baird Stupid, am I? There's the pot calling the kettle black, is it no? Och, do you think I know nothing about women? I've learnt by bitter experience. I've fought three duels over women. I've turned down twelve women——

Flora And just how many have turned *you* down?

Baird Nine—if you must know. Oh, yes, I've been through it all, madam! I've sat and sighed and wrote poetry all day—I've sworn to kill myself for love—written letters ten pages long—I've stood under windows at night in the pouring rain, playing the pipes! But thank you, no more! I've had enough—beautiful eyes, soft shining lips, delightful figures, lilting voices—I tell you, I wouldn't give you sixpence for the lot of them! All women, present company *possibly* excepted, are cheats, hypocrites, jealous, vain, merciless, liars, unreasonable, illogical—and as far as this goes (*he taps his forehead*) they've nothing there. Oh, they can turn on the charm and flirt and flatter when it suits them, but underneath— they're crocodiles, madam. Crocodiles who weep to show how soft and tender they are, but if you let them take you in, they bite where it hurts most. And they can find the best places, believe you me! Tell me honestly, have you ever met a woman who wasn't like that? Have you?

Flora Well, I...

Baird Of course you haven't. They'll always let a man down. I'd trust a Sassenach sooner than any woman!

Flora So—as far as you're concerned—who makes the most faithful and thoughtful lover? Surely not the man?

Baird Ay, that he does.

Flora The *man*? Ha! The *man*!? Since you are determined to stay, let me tell you about the man who did me the honour of marrying me. Now I loved him with all my heart and soul. I did everything I could for him. I made a home for him. I was happy to do so. I never complained or criticised. And how did he repay me? I'll tell you. He came home drunk, reeking of perfume, night after night—if he came at him he flew into a temper and if he could stand upright long enough and see clearly enough—he would strike me. He begrudged every penny he was obliged to give me and criticised the way I spent it—when he *had* any money to give me. Yet, he was my husband and I loved him—since that was my duty. But what hurt me the most was his unfaithfulness—even if I couldn't understand who, apart from me, could be fool enough to fall for his lies. There was a man for you! But now he is dead I will be faithful to him as I was in life. You see, I, a woman, know how to behave as a wife even if he didn't as a husband. That is why I shall stay in mourning for ever.

Baird Pull the other one. I know your game, lassie.

Flora Game? What game?

Baird Oh, come on. I'm no soft in the head no me!

Flora What do you mean by that?

Baird Is it no a fact that you're playing the lovely, lonely widow a bit overmuch? I've no doubt there's a whole procession of young men out there in the street, every day, gazing up at your window—"Oh, puir wee hen. Sitting up there alone after he gave her such a terrible time. *I* could make her happy". Ay, it's a gae old dodge, is that.

Flora Dodge?

Baird Ay, that's the word. Look, if you've really given up the world—why do you still wear make-up and do your hair so prettily?

Flora (*shouting*) How dare you speak to me like that!!?

Baird Would you please lower your voice. It's no very good manners.

Flora You are the last person to talk about manners. You will leave my house at once.

Baird Guid. So you've decided to pay, have you?

Flora No, I have *not*!

Baird Then I'm not going.

Flora I've said my last word on the subject.

Baird A woman's last word? That's a laugh!

Flora (*shouting*) Get out! Get out!!

Baird Will you stop shouting at me—I'm no your husband!

Flora But you can't stay here alone with me—think of my reputation in the neighbourhood.

Baird Your reputation? I'd no thought of that. Thank you.

If a practical casement window is used, Baird draws the curtains and opens both window panes to shout through, otherwise he mimes the action DC and shouts straight at the audience

My name is Andrew Baird and I'm up here alone with Mrs Neil McNeil, the well-known widow. (*He goes back to her*) Now will you pay?

Flora You might as well have saved your breath to cool your porridge. They're all away to Rothesay.

Baird Very well. (*He sits on the* chaise longue)

Flora Please *go*!

Baird Please *pay*!

Flora For the last time—*go*!

Baird For the last time—*no*!

Flora Very well. You leave me with no alternative. I detest violence but it seems to be my only course of action. Leckie!

Leckie enters UL

Leckie You called, madam?

Flora I did. Leckie—throw this gentleman out!

Leckie Mr Baird, sir, if you'd no mind—would you please step this way and I'll see you out—please—thank you.

Baird What did you say, you horrible little man you?

Leckie Jings, madam. He's too much for me!

Flora (*shouting*) Hamish! Dougal! Rory! Help!!

Leckie It's no use, madam—they've gone with Cook to Rothesay.

Flora Oh—damn Rothesay! And as for you, Leckie—you're as much use as paper trews in a thunderstorm!

Leckie Och, madam. (*He lingers near the door*)

Baird You're a wee bit hard on the puir old man, are ye no?

Flora And as for you—I've had quite enough of you too! Andrew Baird—The Bear, forsooth! You're no a bear—you're a bore and a bully. You—you great big Jessie!

Baird What did you call me?

Flora A great big Jessie.

Baird May I ask what gives you the right to insult me?

Flora It wasn't an insult. It was a statement of fact.

Baird Now don't you go thinking that just because you're a woman, I'm not tempted to give you the good hiding you're asking for. If you were a man I'd challenge you to a duel for calling me that.

Flora I'm as good as any man. I accept your challenge. I'm no afraid of you.

Baird Are ye no?

Flora No, I'm not. Let's fight. With pistols. Now!

Leckie Jings!

Flora Hold your weesht, Leckie! Yes, pistols. My husband has a pair.

Baird Now, hold on, hold on! I'm no a hasty man—and I've no wish to fight a woman. I'll accept an apology.

Flora Jessie! (*She slaps his face*)

Baird Right. That does it. You want to be treated as an equal, then, my God, ye will be!

Flora Good. I'll get the pistols. I can't wait to put a bullet through your thick head!

Flora exits UR

Leckie Sir! Sir! Ye'll no do it—for Heaven's sake. Surely you couldn't do it. Please go—don't do it.

Baird Why not? They're ay on about equal rights. Well that's just fine by me. She has an equal right to get herself shot! (*He suddenly laughs*) But did you hear her? "I'll put a bullet through your thick head." Ha, I've never met a woman like her. She's got a lot of nerve. Did you see how her eyes were shining? Her cheeks were glowing—and I love the way she walks. Och, she's a fine woman.

Leckie Please go now, before it's too late. You'll likely be sorry later.

Baird Ay, a fine woman—there's fire in her belly—she's a sonsie lass. It's a shame to shoot her really.

Leckie Then go now, while you've the chance.

Baird No, I couldn't go now. I want to see her again. Now she's gone I miss her already. I *like* that woman. She's mebbe a bit daft to mourn for that louse of a husband—but it shows she's got heart as well as spirit. Yes, I *do* like her. I'm not even sure I want the money now. And, good Lord look at me—I'm *not* in a temper. What a woman!!

Flora enters UR

Flora I've got the pistols. Now, there's one wee thing—I've never fired one of these in my life. Before we fight, would you be so good as to show me what I have to do? If it's no too much trouble?

Baird It will be a pleasure, Mrs McNeil.

Leckie You're mad—the pair of ye. I'll awa' for some help.

Leckie exits UL

Baird Oh, these are fine pistols. And both fully loaded? Oh, take my advice—never leave pistols loaded—you don't want anyone getting hurt, do you?

Flora No, of course not. Thank you for the advice.

Baird Not at all. Oh, yes, these are beauties. They must have cost your old man a pretty penny.

Flora I bought them for him. A wedding anniversary present.

Baird Well now. Take the gun in your right hand like this. Och, your hand is a wee bit small—are you sure you can manage?

Flora I'll do my best, Mr Baird.

Baird I'm sure you will, I'm sure you'll do fine. Now, stand like this—you present less of a target, you see. Now take aim carefully—you have to get this wee thing in the middle of that one—right. Now I usually aim betwen the eyes but you'll do better to aim at me here, (*he taps his chest*) then you'll be like to hit somewhere, high or low. (*He stands behind her, and has to put his arms round her to help her to hold the pistol and aim it*) Now, head up. Support your gun arm with the other hand, like so—then you squeeze the trigger—that's this thing here—squeeze gently—you musn'a pull at it or as it goes off the gun will jerk all over the place and you'll miss me by a mile—and you don't want to do that, do you? Just keep cool and steady—and if you're trembling at all (*he is certainly trembling by now*) ay, trembling the least bit—take a deep breath and it'll likely pass.

Flora (*unsteadily*) Thank you very much.

Baird Not at all. It's the least I can do.

They break apart

Flora Right. Let's go into the garden. I'd rather not fight in here. There's like to be an awful mess, is there not?

Baird Ay, most like. After you, madam. But before we start, I must warn you—and I mean it—when we fight—I fully intend to fire into the air.

Flora May I ask why, sir?

Baird Because—because—I have my reasons. I prefer to keep them to myself.

Flora Isn't that typical of a man? Just now, when you were so helpful and considerate, I began to see a much more attractive side to your character. Now I see you were just humouring the little woman. I suppose you consider it below your dignity to fight against a woman properly. Or are you so sure I'll miss, that you decided to patronise me? OR are you really frightened to fight and you're hoping to trick *me* into firing in the air as well?

Baird All right, all right—yes, I'm afraid. I'm terrified.

Flora Away! You're a terrible liar. There's no way an ex-regimental Sergeant Major in the Black Watch would be afraid. Why are you determined to humiliate me like this? (*She is in tears*) Why won't you shoot at me? *I* want to blow your silly head off!!

Baird Don't cry, for goodness sakes! If you must know—I won't fire at you because I *like* you!

Flora Oh, you do, do you? And what am I supposed to do now? Fling myself into your arms or just kneel at your feet and thank you? You're not getting out of it as easily as that! Come *on*!

Baird I'm sorry if I've upset you—but I'm telling the truth—look, I don't know how to put this, but is it my fault if I'm fond of you? I didn't want it to happen—but you'll just have to face facts. God woman—I'm *more* than fond of you—DAMMIT! I LOVE YOU!! (*He bangs the* DL *chair down, breaking it*)

Flora Look what you've done now. That was his chair.

Baird Then it was rotten—just like he was.

Flora Och. You're impossible! Come away out and get yourself shot!!

Baird Oh, it's true—you're unique—I'm lost—I'm done for. You've caught me for life!

Flora Keep back or I fire!
Baird Fire then. I'd die happily at your feet! It would be an honour
to be shot by you! But all the same I'd be even happier to go on
living—with you. I'm a rich man—even if you don't pay me what
you owe me—I live alone in a large house—a muckle larger than
this one, too—so—will you be my wife?
Flora I think I'd prefer to shoot you. You said you'd die happy.
Bully! Coward!! (*Hopefully*) Jessie?
Baird No, it's no use. I love you as I've never loved before. I've
turned down twelve women——
Flora And nine have turned you down——
Baird Ay, but I never loved one of them at all. I only thought I did.
On my knees I offer you my hand—and my money—and you can
even forget what you owe me. What do you say? Yes or no?
Flora Go away.
Baird You don't want me. Very well. (*He picks up the gun*) I shall
go out and shoot myself. (*He moves towards the door* UL)
Flora (*as he reaches the door*) Stop!
Baird Ay?
Flora Nothing. Go on. Shoot yourself. I don't care. I hate you. Go
on, shoot yourself and deny me the pleasure.

He turns away again

No! Stop! (*She levels the pistol at him*) Put down that pistol.

He does

Now go. I couldn't shoot straight now anyway—I'm shaking that
much. (*She puts her pistol down*)
Baird Ay, I'm shaking too. (*He moves slowly towards her*)
Flora What are you doing? Keep away! Don't you come any
nearer! Keep away!!
Baird I love you—och, how much I love you!
Flora Do stop.

He takes her in his arms

Oh, do stop... Do st... Do ... do... Let's fight... Let's...

They kiss

Leckie enters UL *with a large frying pan*

Leckie Oh... Jings!
Flora Oh, Leckie—for goodness sake—go to Rothesay!!

The CURTAIN *falls*
or
Black-out

FURNITURE AND PROPERTY LIST

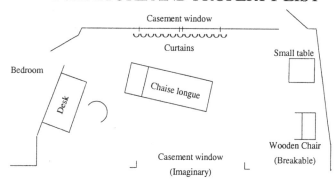

On stage: Desk. *On it*: photograph in heavy black frame
Chaise longue
Small table. *On it*: cup, saucer, plate
Curtains on casement window (optional)
Breakable wooden chair

Off stage: Whisky (**Leckie**)
2 pistols (**Flora**)
Large frying pan (**Leckie**)

Personal: **Baird:** note

LIGHTING PLOT

Property fittings required: nil
1 interior setting. The same throughout

To open: Hot summer afternoon lighting through curtained windows
effect

Cue 1   **Baird** opens curtains   (Page 9)
Bring up afternoon lighting to full

Cue 2   **Flora**: "…go to Rothesay!!"   (Page 15)
Black-out

EFFECTS PLOT

Cue 1   **Flora**: "That will do, Leckie!"   (Page 2)
           Doorbell rings